cutting board

cast iron skillet

measuring cups/spoons

casserole dish

slotted spatula

Measurement Guide

tsp.	teaspoon
tbsp.	tablespoon
c.	
qt.	
oz.	
lb.	pound

D1307079

COOL KIDS COOK

"A pint-sized culinary phenomenon!"
—*New Orleans Times-Picayune*

"I predict you will be a big success."
—Chef Rocco DiSpirito

Kid Chef Eliana grew up in a family of cooks. With grandparents from Cajun Louisiana, the Philippines, Cuba, and Honduras, Eliana's recipes have international flair. She loves traveling and spending time in the kitchen with her family. Eliana says, "Cooking is so much fun. You can be creative and invent new recipes."

At ten years old, Kid Chef Eliana was chosen as one of thirteen Latinos profiled in a museum exhibit at the Southern Food and Beverage Museum in New Orleans. She is a featured kid chef on ZisBoomBah.com, a national Web site for kid foodies. She has cooked with celebrity Chef John Besh and has been a featured chef at many festivals, including the New Orleans Seafood Festival, the Louisiana Book Festival, and the French Market Creole Tomato Festival.

Kid Chef Eliana's mission is to educate kids and inspire them to explore new foods, because good food is more than chicken nuggets and French fries. Her motto is "Cool kids cook and get creative in the kitchen!"

COOL KIDS COOK

Louisiana

by Kid Chef Eliana

with Dianne de Las Casas

Illustrated by Soleil Lisette

PELICAN PUBLISHING COMPANY

GRETNA 2013

Introduction

Hey Young Chefs!

Louisiana is a state rich with music, culture, scenery, and—of course—food. From the moss-draped bayous to the iron-laced balconies of the French Quarter, Louisiana has so much history and tradition, especially in its cuisine.

This cookbook will take you on a culinary journey throughout Louisiana. You will taste delicious Natchitoches meat pies from central Louisiana, savory boudin balls from southwest Louisiana, traditional bouille custard from the Cajun swamps, and sweet Mardi Gras king cake from colorful New Orleans.

I have simplified many of the recipes to make them easier and safer for you to cook for your family and friends. For instance, foods that are traditionally deep-fried are oven-baked. Be sure to work with a grown-up in the kitchen if you feel as if you need help, and remember: safety first!

The cookbook begins with basics that are the foundation for many of the recipes in this book. The cooking utensils you will need as well as an abbreviation guide for measurements are included in the front and back endpapers. Definitions for cooking terms you may not know are located in the glossary at the end of the book.

With the recipes in this cookbook, you will be able to prepare an entire meal for your family. Have fun and *laissez les bon temps rouler*—let the good times roll! Cool kids cook and get creative in the kitchen!

Bon Appétit!

Kid Chef Eliana

Creole Seasoning (KREE-ole)
Makes 1½ cups

Ingredients

2 tbsp. salt
2 tbsp. onion powder
2 tbsp. garlic powder
2 tbsp. dried oregano leaves
2 tbsp. dried sweet basil
1 tbsp. dried thyme leaves

1 tbsp. black pepper
1 tbsp. white pepper
1 tbsp. cayenne pepper
1 tbsp. celery seed
5 tbsp. sweet paprika

Directions

1. Mix thoroughly in a large bowl.
2. Use immediately or store in spice bottle or jar. This recipe can be doubled.

Remoulade Sauce (RUM-uh-lod)
Makes about 1 cup

Ingredients

⅔ c. mayonnaise
1 tbsp. Creole mustard
2 tsp. ketchup
1 tbsp. lemon juice
1 tbsp. celery, finely chopped
1 green onion, finely chopped

1 tbsp. fresh parsley, finely chopped
Dash cayenne pepper
Dash ground black pepper

Directions

1. Mix all ingredients thoroughly in a medium-sized bowl.
2. Use immediately or refrigerate in an airtight container for up to one week.

Roux (ROO)

Makes about ¼ cup

Ingredients

¼ c. cooking oil or butter
¼ c. flour

Chef's Note

Roux is the foundation of many Louisianian dishes, including gumbo, jambalaya, red beans and rice, and soups. There are four basic kinds of roux: white, blond, brown, and dark, each differing in color. This recipe is for a brown roux.

Directions

1. In a sauté pan, heat oil or butter on medium heat.
2. Add flour and stir constantly until smooth and thick. It should be the color of peanut butter.
3. Either use immediately or, once cool, store in an airtight container for up to two weeks in the refrigerator.

Trinity

Makes 4-5 cups

Ingredients

1 large bell pepper
1 large onion
2 medium stalks celery

Directions

1. Finely chop all ingredients.
2. Mix together in a medium-sized bowl.
3. Use immediately or refrigerate in an airtight container for up to three days.

Main Dishes

Barbecue Shrimp	10
Blackened Redfish	13
Chicken and Sausage Gumbo	14
Crab Cakes	17
Jambalaya	18
Muffuletta	21
Natchitoches Meat Pie	22
Pastalaya	25
Pecan-Crusted Fish	26
Red Beans and Rice	29
Roast Beef Po-Boy	30
Shrimp Étouffée	33

Barbecue Shrimp

Serves 4–6

Ingredients

1 qt. water
¼ c. salt
2½ lb. jumbo shrimp
2 sticks butter, melted
2 tbsp. Worcestershire sauce
3 cloves garlic, finely chopped
2 tbsp. lemon juice

2 tbsp. Creole seasoning (see Basics)
¼ c. ginger ale
4-6 servings of angel hair pasta, cooked according to package directions

Directions

1. Preheat oven to 350 degrees.
2. Combine water and salt in a large bowl. Soak the shrimp in the salt-water mixture for 30 minutes.
3. In a medium-sized bowl, combine butter with the Worcestershire sauce.
4. Mix in garlic, lemon juice, Creole seasoning, and ginger ale to butter mixture.
5. Arrange shrimp on a large casserole dish. Pour the sauce over the shrimp.
6. Bake uncovered for 30 minutes.
7. Serve with angel hair pasta.

Chef's Note

Barbecue shrimp is said to have been invented in a New Orleans restaurant, Pascal's Manale. As you see, barbecue shrimp is not really barbecued. It is called that because of the color of the butter sauce.

Barbecue Shrimp

Blackened Redfish

Blackened Redfish

Serves 4

Ingredients

4 8-10 oz. ½-inch redfish fillets
4 tbsp. Creole seasoning (see Basics)
3 sticks butter, melted

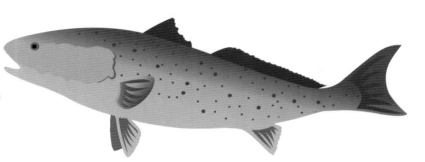

Directions

1. Coat fish fillets with Creole seasoning.
2. Heat a medium-sized iron skillet over high heat until skillet is very hot.
3. Pour melted butter into pan.
4. Using tongs, place fish on the hot butter. Fry fish until black or dark brown on both sides, usually 2-3 minutes per side.

Chef's Note

The blackening technique was created by New Orleans chef Paul Prudhomme. You can also blacken other kinds of meat, such as chicken or beef.

Chicken and Sausage Gumbo (GUM-bo)

Serves 4–6

Ingredients

2 tbsp. olive oil
4 boneless, skinless
   chicken breasts, cubed
½ tsp. salt
¼ tsp. pepper
1 tsp. Creole seasoning,
   or to taste (see Basics)
1 lb. andouille or smoked
   sausage, cut into ½-inch rounds

¼ c. roux (see Basics)
2 c. trinity (see Basics)
2 tbsp. garlic, minced
6 c. chicken stock
2 bay leaves
½ tsp. ground thyme
4-6 servings of rice, cooked
   according to package directions

Directions

1. In a medium-sized skillet over medium-high heat, brown chicken in olive oil with salt, pepper, and Creole seasoning.
2. Add sausage and brown. Set aside.
3. In a large pot over medium heat, heat roux. Add trinity and garlic and stir constantly for about 4 minutes.
4. Add chicken stock, bay leaves, thyme, chicken, and sausage to the pot. Bring to a boil.
5. Cover and cook over medium-low heat for 1 hour. Skim fat.
6. Serve over a cup of rice.

Chef's Note

The secret to a good gumbo is a great roux, which adds a rich flavor. Gumbo is great for serving large groups and tastes even better the next day!

14

Chicken and Sausage Gumbo

Crab Cakes

Crab Cakes

Serves 6–8

Ingredients

1 c. trinity (see Basics)
3 cloves garlic
1 tsp. olive oil
2 tsp. lemon juice
16 oz. crab leg, finely chopped

1 tsp. Creole or Dijon mustard
½ c. mayonnaise
1 c. Italian bread crumbs
Salt and pepper to taste

Directions

1. Preheat oven to 350 degrees. Grease a large baking sheet and set aside.
2. In a food processor, purée trinity and garlic until smooth. Add olive oil and lemon juice.
3. Combine mixture with crab meat in a large bowl. Add mustard, mayonnaise, bread crumbs, salt, and pepper. Mix thoroughly.
4. Shape into small patties with a 3-inch diameter and place on baking sheet.
5. Bake for 20 minutes.
6. Serve on a bed of lettuce or use patty in a sandwich.

Chef's Note

Invented in Maryland, crab cakes were a way for families to have a small amount of seafood feed more people by adding extra ingredients. Crab cakes make a great appetizer but can also be a main course.

Jambalaya

(jum-buh-LIE-yuh)

Serves 4–6

Ingredients

1 tbsp. olive oil
1 c. trinity (see Basics)
1 tbsp. garlic, minced
1 lb. andouille or smoked
   sausage, cut into ½-inch rounds

1 15-oz. can diced tomatoes
½ tsp. salt
¼ tsp. hot sauce
1 c. water
1 c. uncooked rice

Directions

1. In a large skillet, heat oil over medium heat. Add trinity, garlic, and sausage, and cook until sausage is brown.
2. Add remaining ingredients and bring to a boil. Reduce heat to low.
3. Cover and simmer for 30 minutes or until liquid is absorbed by rice.

Chef's Note

Jambalaya is a Creole dish brought by the Spanish to New Orleans in the eighteenth century. It is a version of the Spanish rice dish called paella (pie-AY-yah).

Jambalaya

Muffuletta

Muffuletta (muff-uh-LOT-uh)

Serves 4

Ingredients

1 loaf Muffuletta bread (or Italian bread)
1 c. olive salad
¼ lb. sliced ham
¼ lb. sliced mortadella or salami cotto

¼ lb. sliced genoa salami
¼ lb. sliced provolone cheese
¼ lb. sliced mozzarella cheese

Directions

1. Preheat oven to 400 degrees.
2. Cut bread in half horizontally.
3. Spread the bottom half of the bread with olive salad and then layer the meats and cheeses.
4. Cover with the top half of the bread.
5. Place in oven for 5 minutes or until cheese is melted.
6. Slice into quarters and serve.

Chef's Note

This submarine-type sandwich originated in New Orleans in the early 1900s at Central Grocery. What makes the muffuletta unique is the round Italian bread and the olive salad.

Natchitoches Meat Pie (NACK-uh-dish)
Yields 12–15 small pies

Ingredients

1 tbsp. roux (see Basics)
2 c. trinity (see Basics)
1 lb. ground pork sausage
1 lb. ground beef
2 tbsp. Creole seasoning (see Basics)

3 tsp. salt
Pinch of garlic powder
1 15-oz. package store-bought, refrigerated pie dough, at room temperature
Non-stick cooking spray

Directions

1. Preheat oven to 350 degrees. Grease a large baking sheet and set aside.
2. Heat roux in a large skillet over medium-low heat.
3. Add trinity and cook until soft.
4. Add meats and brown. Stir in Creole seasoning, salt, and garlic powder. Drain fat and cool.
5. On a lightly floured surface, roll out dough to ¼-inch thickness. Use a 5-inch round cookie cutter or a large cup to make a circle of dough.
6. Place a heaping tablespoon of meat mixture in the center of a round. Fold dough over filling so that the pie looks like a half-moon. Seal edges closed by pressing with a fork. Repeat with remaining dough and meat, re-rolling dough scraps as needed.
7. Prick holes into the pies with a fork and spray with non-stick cooking spray.
8. Bake meat pies on baking sheets for 15 to 20 minutes or until golden brown.

Chef's Note

Traditional Natchitoches meat pies are deep fried in peanut oil. In Natchitoches, Louisiana, I ate at Lasyone's (LASS-ee-yo-nes), a restaurant famous for their meat pies. I talked to the chefs, but they wouldn't give up their secret recipe!

Natchitoches Meat Pie

Pastalaya

Pastalaya (pas-tuh-LIE-yuh)
Serves 6–8

Ingredients

1 lb. boneless, skinless
chicken breast, cubed
1 lb. andouille or smoked
sausage, cut into ½-inch rounds
2 tbsp. butter
2 c. trinity (see Basics)
2 cloves garlic, minced

2 c. tomatoes, diced
1 c. chicken broth
2 tbsp. Creole seasoning, plus extra to taste (see Basics)
1 lb. linguine pasta, cooked according to
package directions
2 green onions, chopped
Salt to taste

Directions

1. In a large pot, brown chicken and sausage in butter over medium-high heat.
Remove from pot and set aside.
2. Add trinity to pot and sauté until softened.
3. Stir in garlic, tomatoes, chicken broth, and Creole seasoning.
4. Return meat to pot and bring to boil.
5. Reduce heat, cover, and simmer for about 15 minutes or until chicken is
cooked through.
6. Add cooked pasta and green onions to pot. Combine thoroughly.
7. Add additional Creole seasoning and salt to taste.

Chef's Note

Pastalaya has the ingredients of jambalaya but
uses pasta instead of rice. It takes less time to
cook than jambalaya and can feed a big, hungry
family, which makes it a perfect mid-week meal.

Pecan-Crusted Fish (puh-CON)

Serves 4

Ingredients

¼ c. pecans
½ c. seasoned breadcrumbs
2 tsp. Creole seasoning
(see Basics)
½ tsp. salt
¼ c. flour

½ c. buttermilk
4 6-oz. tilapia fillets (or any
thin, mild white fish)

Directions

1. Preheat oven to 350 degrees. Grease a baking sheet and set aside.
2. Place pecans, breadcrumbs, Creole seasoning, and salt in a food processor and pulse.
3. Pour flour, buttermilk, and pecan mixture onto separate plates. Coat each fish fillet in the flour, then the buttermilk, and then the pecan mixture.
4. Bake on the prepared baking sheet for 10 minutes or until fish is tender and flaky.
5. Serve over a bed of lettuce or with a side salad.

Chef's Note

The pecan is actually a drupe, a fruit with a single pit surrounded by a husk. Pecans have a naturally nutty, buttery flavor and taste best when toasted. I have pecan trees in my backyard!

Pecan-Crusted Fish

Red Beans and Rice

Red Beans and Rice

Serves 6–8

Ingredients

1 lb. red kidney beans
2 qts. water, plus more as needed
1 c. trinity (see Basics)
3 cloves garlic, chopped
4 bay leaves
½ lb. bacon, chopped
1 lb. smoked sausage,
   cut into ½-inch rounds

1 lb. ham, cut into ½-inch cubes
2 tbsp. Creole seasoning,
   or as needed (see Basics)
¼ c. roux (see Basics)
   Salt to taste
   Rice, cooked according to
   package directions

Directions

1. Place beans in a large pot and cover with 2 qts. water. Soak for 4 hours.
2. Add trinity, garlic, and bay leaves to beans and boil until vegetables are tender, about 1 hour.
3. In a skillet, fry bacon until crisp. Add to beans and vegetables.
4. Add smoked sausage and ham to beans. Cook for 1 hour.
5. As the water evaporates, add 1 tablespoon of Creole seasoning for every 4 cups of water you need to add to beans to maintain level of liquid.
6. Add roux to beans and stir well. Beans should have a creamy gravy.
7. Add salt to taste and serve over rice.

Chef's Note

Red beans and rice is traditionally eaten on Mondays. Ham used to be the main dish of a Sunday meal, and leftovers were put into the red beans on Monday, which was wash day. The women did laundry while the dish simmered all day.

29

Roast Beef Po-Boy

Serves 4–6

Ingredients

3 tbsp. Creole seasoning (see Basics)
2 tbsp. salt
1 4-5 lb. bottom round roast, untrimmed
2 c. trinity (see Basics)
3 medium carrots, halved
12 cloves garlic, peeled
   Brown paper bag with no print
12 c. beef stock

4 tbsp. flour
4 tbsp. water
3 12-inch loaves of French bread,
   cut in half horizontally
   Favorite sandwich condiments, such as
   mayonnaise, lettuce, tomatoes,
   and pickles

Directions

1. Preheat oven to 350 degrees.
2. Thoroughly rub Creole seasoning and salt on roast.
3. Scatter trinity, carrots, and garlic in the bottom of large roasting pan.
4. Place roast inside paper bag and wrap bag around roast. Place in pan, tucking end of bag under roast.
5. Pour beef stock into pan until it covers three-quarters of the bag.
6. Cook in oven for 5 hours or until roast falls apart.
7. Remove roast from roasting pan and remove paper. Shred meat.
8. In a small bowl, mix flour and water until smooth. Add to the juices in the roasting pan to thicken into a gravy.
9. Place the shredded roast back into gravy.
10. Place large portions of roast beef on the French bread, along with your favorite sandwich condiments. Traditionally, New Orleans po-boys are "dressed" with mayonnaise, lettuce, tomatoes, and pickles.

Chef's Note

Po-boy is short for "poor boy," an oversized sandwich invented in the late 1920s in New Orleans by Bennie and Clovis Martin. Since then, po-boys have become a Louisiana classic. Roasting the beef in a paper bag makes the meat super tender.

Roast Beef Po-Boy

Shrimp Étouffée

Shrimp Étouffée (eh-too-FAY or ay-too-FAY)

Serves 6–8

Ingredients

2 tbsp. butter
5 green onions, chopped
1 c. trinity (see Basics)
8 oz. tomato sauce
¼ c. ginger ale
2 tsp. favorite seasoning salt

1 tsp. Creole seasoning (see Basics)
½ c. heavy cream
½ c. water plus 1 tbsp.
1 lb. small Louisiana shrimp, peeled and deveined
1 tbsp. cornstarch
Rice, cooked according to package directions

Directions

1. Melt butter in a large pot on medium heat.
2. After butter is melted, add green onions, trinity, tomato sauce, ginger ale, seasoning salt, and Creole seasoning. Stir.
3. Add heavy cream and ½ c. water.
4. After simmering 4-5 minutes, add shrimp.
5. In small bowl, mix together cornstarch and 1 tbsp. water. When étouffée returns to a simmer, pour in cornstarch mixture slowly while stirring.
6. When liquid starts to bubble and shrimp are pink and plump (about 3-5 minutes), serve over rice.

Chef's Note

The word *étouffée* is French for *smothered.* My Nana tought me how to cook yummy étouffée. This is a variation on her recipe.

Side Dishes

Boudin Balls	36
Cajun Boiled Red Potatoes	39
Corn and Crab Bisque	40
Dirty Rice	43
Maque Choux	44
Oven-"Fried" Green Tomatoes	47
Skillet Cornbread	48

Boudin Balls (BOO-dan)

Serves 3–4

Ingredients

½ c. all-purpose flour
 2 large eggs, beaten
½ c. seasoned bread crumbs
12 oz. boudin, about 2 links
    Remoulade sauce, for serving (see Basics)

Directions

1. Preheat oven to 350 degrees. Grease a large baking sheet and set aside.
2. Place flour, eggs, and bread crumbs into separate bowls.
3. Squeeze the inside of the boudin from their casings and crumble. Shape into balls with a 1½-inch diameter.
5. Coat each ball with flour and then eggs. Gently roll each ball in the bread crumbs.
6. Place on the prepared baking sheet. Bake for 30 minutes.
7. Serve with remoulade sauce.

Chef's Note

Boudin is a Cajun "sausage" typically filled with a variety of meats and rice. Legend has it that explorers Louis and Clark ate boudin made by the French fur trapper Toussaint Charbonneau.

Boudin Balls

Cajun Boiled Red Potatoes

Cajun Boiled Red Potatoes

Serves 6–8

Ingredients

5 qts. water
7 tbsp. Creole seasoning
   (see Basics)
2 tsp. garlic powder
2 tbsp. sea salt
⅛ tsp. nutmeg

⅛ tsp. ginger
⅛ tsp. allspice
½ large white onion, diced
10 medium red potatoes, quartered

Directions

1. Fill a large pot with water, Creole seasoning, garlic powder, sea salt, nutmeg, ginger, allspice, and onion. Bring to a boil.
2. Add potatoes and boil until tender, about 20 minutes.
3. Let sit in pot for 10 minutes to absorb flavor.
4. Strain and serve hot.

Chef's Note

During a crawfish boil, it is common to have red potatoes, corn, and onions in the pot with the crawfish. The spicy potatoes and corn are a delicious side dish. This is a great way to add that flavor to a meal without having an entire crawfish boil.

Corn and Crab Bisque (BISK)

Serves 6–8

Ingredients

1 15-oz. can corn
1 c. trinity (see Basics)
3 tbsp. butter
3 tbsp. flour
2 c. chicken or seafood broth
1 c. heavy cream

1 c. milk
2 tsp. Creole seasoning
   (see Basics)
12 oz. crab meat, finely
   chopped

Directions

1. Purée corn and trinity in a food processor or blender.
2. In a large pot, make a blond roux by mixing butter and flour over medium heat only until it turns a beige color.
3. Add the broth, heavy cream, and milk.
4. Stir in the purée and Creole seasoning.
5. Simmer until thickened, about 10 minutes.
6. Add the crab and simmer for 5 more minutes. Serve hot.

Chef's Note

I like to go crabbing with my family. We catch blue crabs, which turn red when they are cooked. Blue crabs are the most harvested crabs in the world because of their tender, sweet meat.

Corn and Crab Bisque

Dirty Rice

Dirty Rice

Serves 6–8

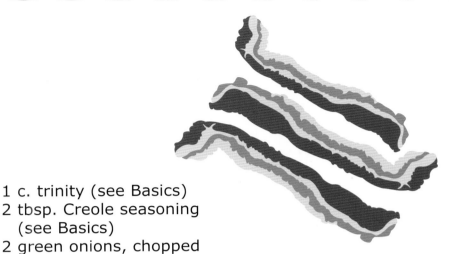

Ingredients

1½ c. long-grain rice
  2 c. chicken broth, divided
  2 c. water
  5 slices bacon, chopped
 ½ lb. ground pork
 ½ lb. ground beef

1 c. trinity (see Basics)
2 tbsp. Creole seasoning
  (see Basics)
2 green onions, chopped
  Salt to taste

Directions

1. Cook rice according to package instructions, using 1 c. chicken broth and 2 c. water for the cooking liquid.
2. While rice is cooking, render the bacon in a large skillet over medium-low heat.
3. Add ground pork and ground beef to the skillet with bacon. Brown meat over high heat.
4. Add trinity. Stir and cook on medium-high heat until soft.
5. Add remaining chicken broth and deglaze pan.
6. Add Creole seasoning and increase to high heat. Reduce most of the chicken stock.
7. Add rice to meat and mix.
8. Turn off heat. Sprinkle with green onions and salt to taste. Serve hot.

Chef's Note

A traditional Cajun dish, dirty rice is called dirty because of its dark color. It is usually made with chicken giblets, but I have created a kid-friendly version by using more common ingredients.

Maque Choux (MOCK shoo)
Serves 4

Ingredients

2 tbsp. butter
½ c. trinity (see Basics)
2 c. corn kernels
  (approximately 3 medium ears
  or 1 15-oz. can)
½ c. diced tomatoes

1 tbsp. Creole seasoning
  (see Basics)
¼ c. heavy cream
Salt to taste

Directions

1. Melt butter in a large skillet over medium-high heat.
2. Add trinity and sauté for 5 minutes.
3. Add corn and sauté for 2 minutes.
4. Add tomatoes, Creole seasoning, and heavy cream. Cover, reduce heat to medium-low, and simmer until sauce thickens, about 30 minutes. Add salt to taste.

Chef's Note

When the Acadians came to Louisiana, corn was not a part of their diet. The local Native Americans introduced them to corn. Cornbread and other tasty corn dishes such as maque choux became part of Cajun cooking.

Maque Choux

Oven-"Fried" Green Tomatoes

Oven-"Fried" Green Tomatoes

Serves 6

Ingredients

 1 c. cornmeal
½ tsp. Creole seasoning (see Basics)
½ tsp. salt
¼ tsp. pepper
 5 medium green tomatoes, sliced
    Remoulade sauce, for serving (see Basics)

Directions

1. Preheat oven to 325 degrees. Lightly grease a medium-sized baking sheet and set aside.
2. In a small bowl, mix the cornmeal, Creole seasoning, salt, and pepper.
3. Dip tomato slices into the mixture, coating both sides. Arrange coated slices in a single layer on the prepared baking sheet.
4. Bake for 45 minutes until crisp and golden brown. Serve with remoulade sauce.

Chef's Note

I love going to a local farmer's market in Belle Chasse, Louisiana, called Becnel's. They have the best Creole tomatoes. These large, meaty tomatoes make the perfect oven-"fried" green tomatoes.

Skillet Cornbread
Serves 6–8

Ingredients

4 tbsp. bacon drippings or
    vegetable oil, divided
2 c. self-rising cornmeal
2 eggs, beaten
2 c. buttermilk
    Dash of cayenne pepper, optional

Directions

1. Preheat oven to 450 degrees.
2. Grease a cast iron skillet with 2 tbsp. bacon drippings or vegetable oil, coating the entire pan.
3. Combine cornmeal, eggs, buttermilk, cayenne pepper, and the remaining 2 tbsp. of bacon drippings or oil in a large bowl. Pour batter into the prepared skillet.
4. Bake for 35 minutes or until golden brown.
5. Cut into 6-8 wedges and serve.

Chef's Note

In the American South, cornbread is often made in an iron skillet. This cornbread recipe is very versatile. You can add bacon, cheese, peppers, or just about any ingredient to make your own version.

Skillet Cornbread

Desserts

Bouille	52
King Cake	55
Pralines	56
Sweet Potato Casserole	59
White Chocolate Bread Pudding	60

Bouille (boo-YEE)
Serves 8-10

Ingredients

1 c. sugar
2 egg yolks
8 heaping tsp. cornstarch
1 12-oz. can evaporated milk
12 oz. heavy cream

½ c. butter
1 tbsp. vanilla extract
Yellow cake or pound cake
and fresh berries, optional

Directions

1. Combine sugar, egg yolks, and corn starch in a small bowl. Set aside.
2. In a large sauce pot over medium heat, heat evaporated milk, heavy cream, and butter. (Hint: use the evaporated milk can to measure the cream.)
3. When the butter is fully melted, add the egg mixture.
4. Add vanilla and whisk until mixture thickens into custard and sticks to the back of a spoon.
5. Serve the custard over a slice of yellow cake or pound cake. Top with fresh berries.

Chef's Note

Bouille is a Cajun custard similar to a crème anglaise. This dish was traditionally served as a dessert or a treat when someone was sick. It is delicious as a topping over cake or just by itself.

Bouille

King Cake

King Cake

Serves 8-10

Ingredients

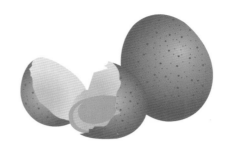

1 packet active dry yeast
¼ c. water, warmed to 105 degrees
2 tbsp. milk, scalded and cooled
4½ c. flour, divided
2 sticks butter, softened, and
2 tsp. butter, melted

¾ c. sugar
¼ tsp. salt
4 eggs
½ c. light corn syrup for topping
2 tbsp. each, purple, green and
yellow colored sugar

Directions

1. Dissolve yeast in water.
2. Add scalded milk and ½ c. flour to yeast mixture.
3. In a large bowl, blend sticks of butter, sugar, salt, and eggs. Add yeast mixture and combine thoroughly.
4. Gradually add 2½ c. flour to make a medium-sized dough. Place in a greased bowl and brush with melted butter. Cover with a damp cloth and let rise until doubled in volume, about 3 hours.
5. Scatter 1 c. flour on a surface and knead dough. Roll into a 4-foot long rope. Form into an oval on a large, greased baking sheet, pinching the ends of the rope together.
6. Cover dough with a damp cloth and let rise until doubled in volume, about 1 hour.
7. Preheat oven to 325 degrees.
8. Bake for 35 to 45 minutes or until lightly browned.
9. When cake is cool, brush the top with corn syrup and sprinkle with purple, green, and yellow colored sugar, alternating colors around the cake.

Chef's Note

The king cake is a Mardi Gras tradition. The Mardi Gras season begins on January 6, the twelfth day of Christmas. The king cake honors the three kings and is decorated in the traditional colors of purple, green, and gold, symbolizing justice, faith, and power.

Pralines (PRAW-leens)

Makes about 2 dozen

Ingredients

2 c. pecans, chopped
1 16-oz. box light brown sugar
1 14-oz. can condensed milk
  Dash salt

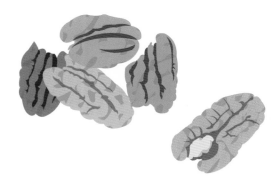

Directions

1. Lightly grease several sheets of wax paper.
2. Place saucepan over medium heat and combine pecans, sugar, condensed milk, and salt. Stirring constantly, bring to a boil.
3. Once boiling, stir for 7 minutes.
4. Remove from heat and use a wooden spoon to beat the mixture for about 3-5 minutes until it begins thickening and no longer looks shiny.
5. Working quickly, use a metal tablespoon to drop the mixture onto wax paper, creating 2-inch wide pralines. Let sit until firm.
6. If there are any leftovers, store in an airtight container between layers of wax paper.

Chef's Note

Pralines were invented in France using almonds, but in the American South we use pecans. In Louisiana, we pronounce pecans as "puh-CONS." I learned how to make pralines from our family friend, Stacey Hensley.

Pralines

Sweet Potato Casserole

Sweet Potato Casserole

Serves 6–8

Ingredients

6 large sweet potatoes, cooked,
  peeled and mashed
1 c. granulated sugar
½ c. butter, melted
½ c. evaporated milk
2 eggs
2 tsp. vanilla extract

For the Topping:
2 c. pecans, chopped
¾ c. brown sugar, packed
1½ c. flour
5 tbsp. butter, melted

Directions

1. Preheat oven to 350 degrees. Coat a 9x13-inch casserole dish with nonstick cooking spray.
2. In a large bowl, mix together sweet potatoes, sugar, butter, evaporated milk,
  eggs, and vanilla.
3. Pour mixture into casserole dish.
4. In a separate bowl, combine the pecans, brown sugar, flour, and butter for the topping.
5. Spread the topping evenly on top of the sweet potato mixture.
6. Bake for 45 minutes. Serve hot.

Chef's Note

Louisiana is one of the largest producers of sweet potatoes in the United States. Sweet potatoes are a type of tuber, an important root vegetable. This is my family's recipe and can be served as a side dish as well.

White Chocolate Bread Pudding
Serves 8–10

Ingredients

6 slices stale French bread,
  broken into pieces
2 tbsp. butter, melted
4 eggs, beaten
2 c. milk
¾ c. granulated sugar

1 tsp. of cinnamon
1 tsp. of vanilla extract
2 c. white chocolate chips
¼ c. sweetened
  condensed milk, optional

Directions

1. Preheat oven to 350 degrees.
2. Place bread in a greased 8-inch square baking pan. Drizzle melted butter on top.
3. In a mixing bowl, combine eggs, milk, sugar, cinnamon, and vanilla. Mix well.
4. Pour mixture over bread.
5. Push bread down until egg mixture is soaked into bread.
6. Mix in white chocolate chips and sprinkle a handful on top of mixture.
7. Bake for 45 minutes or until golden brown. Serve with a drizzle of
   sweetened condensed milk.

Chef's Note

The tradition of bread pudding was brought to the America from Europe. Instead of tossing out old bread, a delicious pudding was made with it. White chocolate bread pudding was invented by Palace Café in New Orleans. Mmm!

White Chocolate Bread Pudding

Glossary of Cooking Terms

Beat—To stir and mix ingredients rapidly.

Boil—To heat a liquid until it bubbles.

Brown—To cook briefly on high heat in hot fat or oil until a crust forms.

Chop—To cut food into uniform pieces.

Dash—A very small measurement of seasoning added with a quick flick of the hand.

Deglaze—To heat a small amount of liquid in a pan while stirring to loosen the brown bits at the bottom of the pan.

Dissolve—To mix a dry ingredient in a liquid until it disappears.

Dollop—A small glob of food.

Dough—A combination of flour, water or milk, and other ingredients that, when cooked, will become a bread or pastry.

Drizzle—To pour a liquid in thin streams.

Evaporate—To change a liquid or solid into a vapor so that it disappears.

Grease—To rub or spray butter or oil on a cooking implement so that food does not stick to it.

Knead—To squeeze dough by pushing, stretching, and folding to mix all ingredients.

Melt—To turn a solid into a liquid by heating.

Mix—To combine ingredients by stirring well.

Packed—Firmly pressed into a measuring cup.

Purée—To mash foods until smooth.

Reduce—To boil down to a smaller volume.

Render—To turn solid fat into liquid by melting slowly.

Roast—To cook in an oven using dry heat.

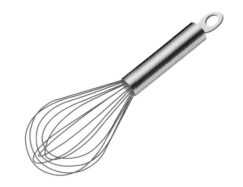

Roux—A cooking mixture of flour and oil or butter used to thicken sauces, soups, and stews. Roux comes in four main colors: white, blond, brown, and dark.

Sauté—To cook food in a small amount of hot fat.

Scald—To heat to a temperature just below the boiling point.

Simmer—To cook slowly in liquid over low heat.

Skim—To remove fat from the surface of a liquid.

Slice—To cut food into even thicknesses.

Sprinkle—To scatter dry ingredients or drops of liquid.

Stir—To mix ingredients in a circular motion.

Strain—To remove solids from liquid, usually using a strainer or a colander.

Whisk—To beat rapidly with an instrument that allows air into a mixture, making it light and frothy. Also the name of a cooking tool used for this purpose.

Acknowledgments

To Mom, Dad, Soleil, Nana, Abuela, and my Cajun Paw Paw. Thank you so much for your love and support!

Special thanks to Nana (Josie Chretien), Paw Paw (Clay Chretien), Uncle Gary James, Christian James, Jourdan James, Camrynn James, Ashlynn James, Jasmynn James, Abuela (Jennie Casas), Aunt Pam Casas, Uncle George Parjus, and Stacey C. Hensley for testing and tasting the recipes.

Library of Congress Cataloging-in-Publication Data

Kid Chef Eliana, 2000-
  Cool kids cook : Louisiana / by Kid Chef Eliana, with Dianne de Las Casas ; illustrated by Soleil Lisette.
    pages cm
  Audience: 8-12
  Audience: Grade 4 to 6
  ISBN 978-1-4556-1762-3 (hardcover : alk. paper) -- ISBN 978-1-4556-1763-0 (e-book) 1. Cooking, American--Louisiana style--Juvenile literature. I. De Las Casas, Dianne. II. Lisette, Soleil, illustrator. III. Title.
  TX715.2.L68K53 2013
  641.59763--dc23
                                        2012030183

Photographs by Stacey C. Hensley
Food styling by Dianne de Las Casas

Printed in Malaysia
Published by Pelican Publishing Company, Inc.
1000 Burmaster Street, Gretna, Louisiana 70053